How to be a Gramma

Written by
Carol Kirk Witbeck

How to be a Gramma
Copyright © 2024 by Carol Kirk Witbeck

ISBN: 979-8895310687 (hc)
ISBN: 979-8895310663 (sc)
ISBN: 979-8895310670 (e)

Writers' Branding
(877) 608-6550
www.writersbranding.com
media@writersbranding.com

How to be a Gramma

By:

Carol Kirk Witbeck

Being a Gramma comes with no rules.

There are no special classes and no special schools.

They don't need to wear armour or invisible capes,

And they naturally come in all sizes and shapes.

They can be short in their stature or even quite tall,

Or dress in a large or maybe a small;

And they come in all colors and come in all shades,

And even in circles or stripes or in plaids.

They're all very different but each stand in awe
When they're first called that wonderful
name of Gramma.

Grammas don't have to make quilts, or stand on stilts.

They don't have to make lunch, with strange purple punch.

They don't have to like sewing, or bowling or hiking:

They don't have to go shopping or even go biking:

They don't have to eat donuts the regular way,
or love to go riding a hill on a sleigh.

They don't have to have rabbits, or kitties or puppies,
Turtles, Plecostomus, snails, or guppies.

They don't have to be smart but there are
things they should know
Like mug-womps, and gribs, and poking bee boes.

And smiling and listening and giving warm hugs,
And knowing how to get rid of really large bugs,

And telling a story when they sit on your lap
Before nodding off and taking a nap.

Grammas, always be grateful for taking a part
Of sharing with someone a place in your heart.
Remember, there's nothing that you need to do
Grammas are already special, so just be you.

Of course, you have to know what mug-womps are and gribs and bee boes.
It also helps to know what a Plecostomus is,
the proper way to eat a donut, and how to get rid of bugs.
But they can easily be explained.

- Plecostomus = a type of fish with a suction mouth that eats the gunk off the glass in an aquarium.

- Mug-womp = a made-up word for a bird on a wire with his mug on one side and his womp on the other.

- Gribs = a made-up word for whiskers.

- Bee boes = a made-up word for belly button (singular is Bee bo).

- A non-regular way to eat a donut is hanging it from a string.

- The best way to get rid of a really large bug is to vacuum it up—whoosh, it's gone and there's no nasty residue.

- Oh, I almost forgot. Being a Gramma is easy, but you must know 101 ways to use a toilet paper roll!